DIPLODOCUS

the DINOSAUR with the...

looong neck

Helen Greathead

Illustrated by Mike Spoor

SCHOLASTIC

Other books in the series:
Iguanodon – the dinosaur with fat bottom
T.Rex – the dinosaur with stupid smile
Stegosaurus – the dinosaur with spiky spine

Professor Michael J Benton – dinosaur consultant
Valerie Wilding – educational advisor
Ben Newth – researcher

Scholastic Children's Books,
Commonwealth House, 1-19 New Oxford Street,
London WC1A 1NU, UK

A division of Scholastic Ltd
London ~ New York ~ Toronto ~ Sydney ~ Auckland
Mexico City ~ New Delhi ~ Hong Kong

Published in the UK by Scholastic Ltd, 2003

Text copyright © Helen Greathead, 2003
Illustrations copyright © Mike Spoor, 2003

ISBN 0 439 97822 X

All rights reserved
Printed and bound by Nørhaven Paperback A/S, Denmark

2 4 6 8 10 9 7 5 3 1

The right of Helen Greathead and Mike Spoor to be identified as author and illustrator
of this work respectively has been asserted by them in accordance with the Copyright,
Designs and Patents Act, 1988.

Contents

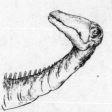

Introduction **5**

Diplodocus and you **6**

Diplodocus sticks
its neck out **14**

Diplodocus changes
the world **27**

Diplodocus never
forgets **36**

Diplodocus dies **48**

Diplodocus starts
some arguments **56**

Introduction

Dinosaur names are often hard to say.
It's easier to say them in bits:

Di-plod-oh-kus

Say it slowly, then a bit faster. Diplodocus.
Now you know the name of a very long
dinosaur.

Diplodocus and you

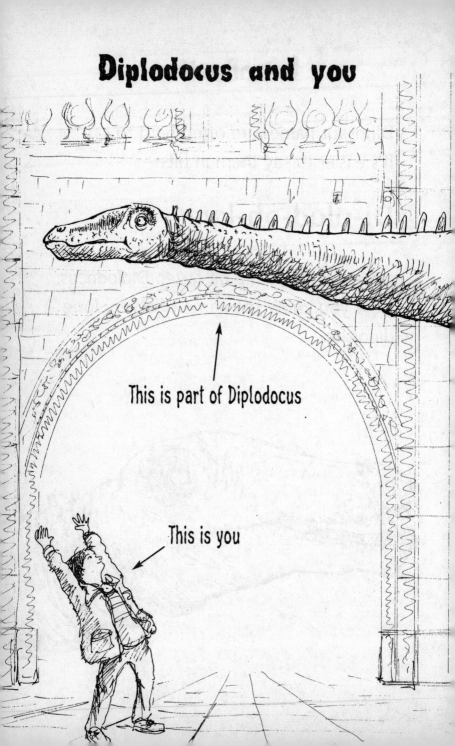

This is part of Diplodocus

This is you

It's difficult to fit you and Diplodocus on the same page. Diplodocus has got a VERY long neck, hasn't it? Some scientists think Diplodocus held its neck straight out in front so its head stayed close to the ground.

Look up and
you can see
another bit of
Diplodocus.
Its body is
nearly ALL
tummy.

Its legs are stubby
and fat.
They have to be
strong to hold up
that huge body.

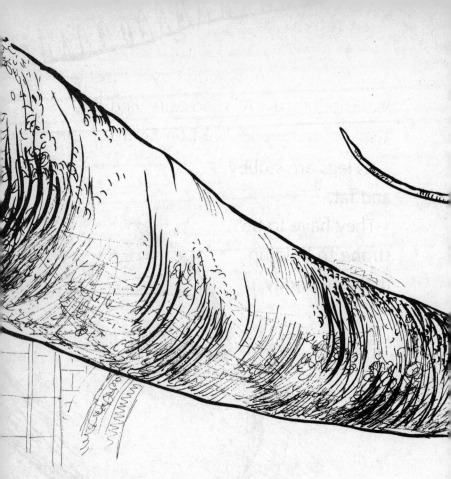

Hanging over your head is the last bit of Diplodocus – its tail. The tail is even longer than the neck. It is thin and bendy. Diplodocus can swish it from side to side, so you'd better watch out!

Of course, you wouldn't ever meet a real Diplodocus. All dinosaurs died out ages before people lived on Earth.

Diplodocus belonged to a group of dinosaurs called sauropods (sore-oh-pods). They were the biggest creatures EVER to walk on Earth. And the longest!

Diplodocus was taller than a giraffe.
It was much bigger than an elephant.
And a lot longer than a python.

Some scientists think it could live for up to 200 years! When a Diplodocus was born, it kept on growing. The older it got, the bigger it grew. So the oldest Diplodocus was absolutely massive.

But why was it so big?

Diplodocus sticks its neck out

There were some good things about being big.

Diplodocus could reach food other creatures couldn't get at.

It could choose its food first.

It didn't have to worry about being attacked.

But there were some bad things about being big, too.

Diplodocus was too heavy to hop, skip, jump or run. It could only walk veeerrry slooowly.

Being heavy meant its bones could crack easily. A cracked bone might mend. But a broken bone meant Diplodocus couldn't move at all. If it didn't move, it couldn't find enough food to feed itself. It would be a dead Diplodocus.

Urk!

Diplodocus had to eat nearly all day to feed its great big body. It had to drink a lot, too. Diplodocus had to keep moving to find food and water. And that's why its long neck was so brilliant…

It could stretch out to reach into a deep, thick forest.

It could reach down into a river to pick out some tasty weeds.

It could gobble up all the leaves and ferns in sight, while the rest of its body stayed put!

But sometimes Diplodocus couldn't
reach the leaves on the taller trees.
So it sat on its back legs and its tail.
Then it lifted its front legs up, and
pushed a whole tree right over!

C-R-E-A-K

Diplodocus looked funny sitting like this.
It was too heavy to move fast. But
Diplodocus was not as heavy as other
sauropods. Its bones were hollow, so they
were light, too. That's why, when
Diplodocus pushed up on to its back legs,
it didn't topple over.

At the end of that very long neck, was a tiny head – with a very small brain. The head of a Diplodocus was not much bigger than your head.

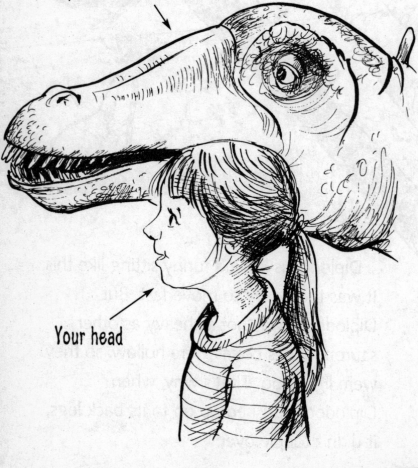

Diplodocus head

Your head

Inside its mouth were some funny, sticky-out teeth. There were only a few of them and they were not very strong. They were long, thin and gappy! But Diplodocus didn't need a dinosaur dentist. Its teeth were like that for a reason.

Diplodocus was a vegetarian dinosaur. It ate almost anything – as long as it was green. When Diplodocus reached up to a tasty looking tree, it opened its mouth and whole branches went in.

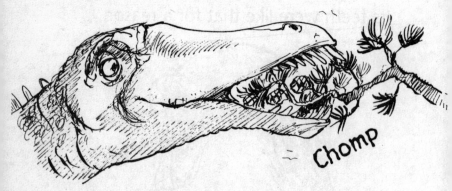

Chomp

It clamped its teeth together and pulled back its head. The pine needles, cones and green twigs stayed in its mouth.

Nibble

The tough branches came out again –
through the gaps in the teeth!

Chomp

Diplodocus probably had green bits stuck
between its teeth a lot of the time.

Burp

Diplodocus only had teeth at the front of its mouth. It didn't have any back teeth to chew its food. Instead, it rolled the food around with its tongue and covered it in spit.

Diplodocus needed loads of spit. It probably dribbled most of the time. But the spit was really useful. It held the food together so it could slide easily all the way down into the tummy. Diplodocus didn't want anything to get stuck in its very long neck.

And Diplodocus
swallowed something
else to help its food
go down ...

Splat!

… stones! Lots of them.

The stones helped Diplodocus to chew
… with its tummy! Strong muscles in a
Diplodocus tum churned the food around.
The stones helped to mush the food into
smaller bits.

As the stones whirled round in the huge
Diplodocus tummy, they started to grind
smooth. When they got really smooth
they were no use any more. So Diplodocus
pooed them out! Then it searched for
some new ones, and started again.

Diplodocus changes
the world

Diplodocus travelled as part of a herd.
Hundreds of them walked together –
very slowly. The herd was very big indeed!
And wherever it went, the land it walked
on would never be the same again.

Other dinosaurs knew when the herd was coming. They heard a rumbling sound, like thunder. The sound was Diplodocuses breathing, burping and thumping the ground as they walked! It got louder as they moved closer. It was quite scary! But at least other animals had plenty of time to get out of the way. They could hear the herd coming ages before they arrived.

The Diplodocuses ate as they went.
They walked up to forests that looked
like this:

And left them behind looking like this:

What a mess! When Diplodocus left a
forest behind, it wasn't really a forest
any more!

But a trampled forest made life easier
for some animals.

Smaller plants grew when the trees
were out of the way. Lots of animals fed
on the smaller plants, and on the tops of
the pushed-over trees.

Meanwhile, Diplodocus kept on moving. Life for the herd was nearly always the same. Walk a bit … then eat a bit. Walk a bit … eat a bit. They didn't have much reason to stop, except, perhaps to have …

... a bath!

Sometimes the herd found huge, muddy puddles of water. They knelt down and rolled over in the mud! The bath didn't make them cleaner, but it was great for their skin. It got rid of niggling insects and it kept Diplodocus cool in the hot sun.

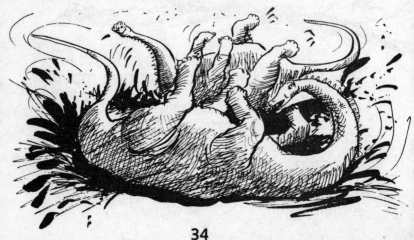

But when the huge, heavy dinosaurs climbed out of their bath, the muddy puddle was different…

They had made it deeper and wider, ready to fill up with rain – and turn the muddy puddle into a nice, deep pool!

Diplodocus never forgets

The herd did everything together. The female Dipodocuses even laid their eggs together.

First they found land with some water nearby. This was their nesting ground.

Then they squatted down. They might lay as many as 40 eggs each!

They covered the eggs with rotten
leaves to keep them warm.

Then they walked off ... and left behind
hundreds and hundreds of eggs.

This was bad news for the Diplodocus eggs. With no adults to guard them, anything could happen! The eggs were only this big:

Diplodocus egg

You

Dipolodocus eggs were great for other dinosaurs to eat. The eggs couldn't run away. And they were full of goodness, too.

Slurp!

So why did the mums leave their babies behind? Well, they had to! A Diplodocus had to keep eating. It had to keep moving to find enough food. If all the mums stayed with their eggs, they would quickly run out of food … and die! And that would not help their babies at all.

So the babies that did hatch out had to find their own food and water. And they were always in danger. The mums laid all those eggs for a good reason. A lot of the eggs got eaten. A lot of the babies got eaten, too. But lots, lots more of them survived.

A newly hatched Diplodocus was not much bigger than a human baby:

Human baby

Diplodocus baby

And next to its mum, baby Dip was ...

... tiny!

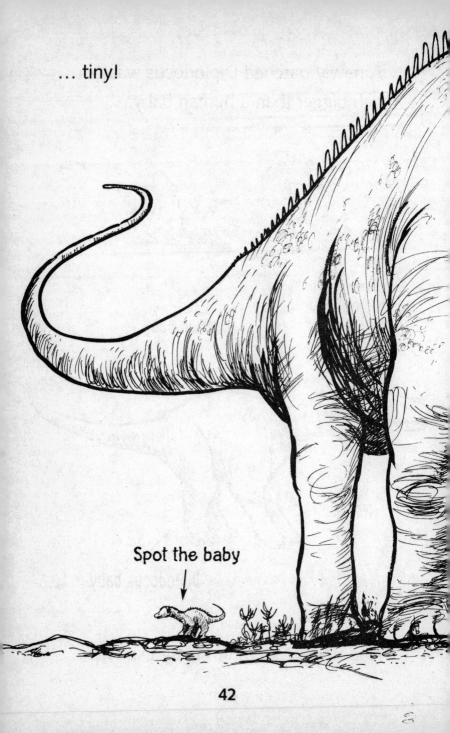

Spot the baby

So why couldn't the baby walk with the herd?

A newborn Diplodocus could not walk from one end of its mum to the other, without stopping for a rest.

It might get crushed under mum's enormous feet!

The herd moved slowly, but baby Dip
could never keep up.

As soon as it hatched out, the baby Diplodocus started eating tasty weeds from the river and ferns from the bank. It had to learn to look after itself quickly. And it needed to eat a lot, because it was about to start growing like mad.

Baby Dip grew bigger
and bigger and bigger.
And just as it was
big enough to
walk with the
herd …

… the mums came back! Did they
remember their babies and come back
for them? Or did they just come back to
lay more eggs? Nobody knows for sure.
But this time, when the herd moved on,
the little ones went, too.

Diplodocus dies

Even with the herd, a young Diplodocus
was not out of danger.

Allosaurus was a meat-eating dinosaur.
It had long, sharp teeth. It had deadly
claws. And Allosaurus liked the taste of
Diplodocus meat.

An Allosaurus might follow the herd, hoping to find a dead Diplodocus.

But if a Diplodocus didn't die by itself, Allosaurus might have to attack it. So Allosaurus hid … and waited. It waited for a young Diplodocus … or a sick Diplodocus, or a very, very old Diplodocus, to trail behind the herd.

A weak Diplodocus could still fight. It could sit back on its legs and tail, and thump down on Allosaurus with its front legs.

Thump

It could jab Allosaurus with the spike on each of its front feet.

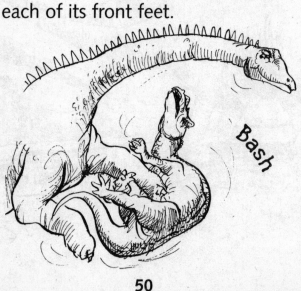

Bash

It could use its tail a bit like a whip ...
to slash through Allosaurus's skin!

Thwack

But a weak Diplodocus got tired
quickly. It was easier for
Allosaurus to kill. And it
was worth the effort.
One Diplodocus
would keep
Allosaurus well
fed for days.

Mmm

Allosaurus was a danger to Diplodocus.
But something else was far more
deadly…

It wasn't another dinosaur. It wasn't
even an animal. Diplodocus was in most
danger from … the weather!

When Diplodocus lived, there were only two seasons – wet and dry.

If the rains started in the north, Diplodocus travelled south. When the rains came in the south, Diplodocus travelled north again.

But sometimes the rains didn't come at all. Without water, the leaves and ferns started to wither and die. The lakes and rivers dried up.

There was nothing to eat or drink. The herd was huge. It took a lot of food to feed all those dinosaurs. When the food died, the dinosaurs died, too – by the hundred. The weather could kill the whole herd.

Diplodocus starts some arguments

Life was tough for Diplodocus. But Diplodocus was a survivor. We know, because there are loads of Diplodocus fossils to prove it. The fossils show that there were once thousands and thousands of Diplodocuses!

Fossils are bones or traces of dinosaurs, like a footprint, or a tail trail, that have turned to rock over millions of years.

Samuel
Williston

A dinosaur hunter called Samuel Williston found the first Diplodocus fossils in 1877, in North America. It was named Diplodocus by dinosaur expert, O.C. Marsh. The name means "double beamed".

O.C. Marsh

The name comes from the strange shape of the bones underneath Diplodocus's tail. The bones looked like this:

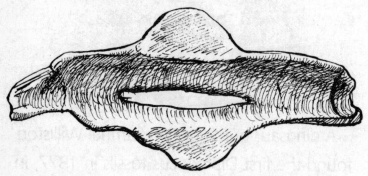

Scientists once thought the bones protected the tail as it trailed along the ground. But now they're not sure what they were for ... because they now know Diplodocus didn't drag its tail at all!

And that's just one Diplodocus fact that scientists have argued about.

In 1899, a millionaire called Andrew Carnegie paid for the fossilized bones of a whole Diplodocus to be put back together again. He displayed the skeleton in his own museum. It was ENORMOUS! Everybody wanted to see it.

Carnegie had a great idea. He sent models of Diplodocus to museums around the world.

But the models were finished in a hurry. And the skeleton had some bones missing. The Diplodocus models ended up with the wrong front feet! They were the back feet of a dinosaur called Camarasaurus!

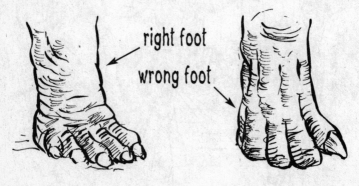

right foot
wrong foot

Scientists wanted to find out more about Diplodocus. But they often got the facts wrong. Some thought Diplodocus was too heavy to walk on land. They said it lived in deep lakes, and that only its eyes and its nostrils poked out of the water – so it could breathe and see!

Other scientists thought this was nonsense! And when fossilized footprints of Diplodocus were found, they finally proved that:

Diplodocus walked on land.
Diplodocus lived with a herd.
Diplodocus didn't drag its tail.

Until just a few years ago, Diplodocus was always shown with its nostrils on the top of its head. Like this:

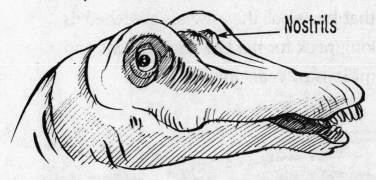

Nostrils

But a scientist, called Lawrence Witmer, did a study of dinosaur noses! He discovered that Diplodocus's nostrils were not on the top of its head, after all. They were just where you'd expect to find them. On the front of its face.

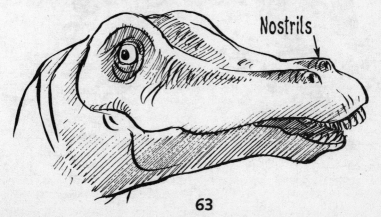

Nostrils

Most scientists now agree that Witmer was right. But there are still lots of things they don't agree on. And the one creature that knows all the answers stretched its long neck for the last time millions and millions of years ago.